FOLENS GEOGRAPHY HIGHLIGHTS

Geography for Infants

John Corn

Contents

Introduction	3
Around the School 1	4
Around the School 2	8
How Can We Make Our Local Area Safer?	12
An Island Home 1	16
An Island Home 2	20
Going to the Seaside 1	24
Going to the Seaside 2	28
Where in the World is Gordon the Gnome?	32
Where in the World are You?	36
Global Eye	40
An Island Overseas	44
Additional Information	48

© 2002 Folens Limited.

United Kingdom: Folens Publishers, Apex Business Centre, Boscombe Road, Dunstable, LU5 4RL.
Email: folens@folens.com

Ireland: Folens Publishers, Greenhills Road, Tallaght, Dublin 24.
Email: info@folens.ie

Poland: JUKA, ul. Renesansowa 38, Warsaw 01-905.

Folens allows photocopying of pages marked 'copiable page' for educational use, providing that this use is within the confines of the purchasing institution. Copiable pages should not be declared in any return in respect of any photocopying licence.

Folens publications are protected by international copyright laws. All rights are reserved. The copyright of all materials in this publication, except where otherwise stated, remains the property of the publisher and author. No part of this publication may be reproduced, stored in a retrieval system, or transmitted, in any form or by any means, for whatever purpose, without the written permission of Folens Limited.

John Corn hereby asserts his moral rights to be identified as the author of this work in accordance with the Copyright, Designs and Patents Act 1988.

Editor: Katherine Jacobson
Layout artist: Suzanne Ward
Cover design: Martin Cross
Cover image: Robert Harding Picture Library –robertharding.com
Illustrations: Gary Clifford

First published 2002 by Folens Limited.
Reprinted 2002.
Reprinted 2003.

Every effort has been made to trace the copyright holders of material used in this publication. If any copyright holder has been overlooked, we should be pleased to make any necessary arrangements.

British Library Cataloguing in Publication Data. A catalogue record for this publication is available from the British Library.

ISBN 1 84303 153-1

Introduction

Geography Highlights presents units from the QCA scheme of work in activities that are accessible to children in the Infant and Junior phases. Through the units selected, **Geography Highlights** focuses on the concepts, skills and knowledge in Geography that enable children to build up referencing and organisational skills relating to any area or topic in Geography as a whole.

Geography for Infants is aimed at children aged 5–7 (Y1/2, P2/3). It highlights units 1–5, 17 and 22 of the QCA scheme of work (see below).

Each unit comprises:

Ideas page
This teacher reference page sets out the essential background to the unit with learning objectives and lesson notes for each activity sheet. There is a section on introducing and using the activity sheet and suggestions for follow-up and extension work. The symbol [F] is used to denote activities involving fieldwork, though it is recognised that in some cases the first-hand experience of a field trip may need to be replaced by or supplemented with information from reference books or on-line sources. A useful reference tool for children's research on the Internet and on-line sources is *Online Geography* by John Lancaster (Belair BA0309). Teachers will also find *Folens Geography Big Books 1 and 2* (F4503 and F4511) provide a valuable resource to support these units.

Activity sheets
The three activity sheets for each of the units aim to provide information, processes and model layout tools for researching, organising and presenting information in Geography. The sheets are designed to be used by children working with the support of a teacher or assistant throughout. Children may work together in small groups or, if they are able, in pairs. It may be helpful to enlarge the activity sheets to A3 size during shared or group-guided work. They may also be projected through an overhead transparency or electronic whiteboard.

Units from the QCA Geography scheme of work covered in *Geography for Infants*
(The coverage in this book is shown in bold beneath the QCA units.)

1 Around our school – the local area **Chapters 1 and 2**	2 How can we make our local area safer? **Chapter 3**	3 An island home **Chapters 4 and 5**	4 Going to the seaside **Chapters 6 and 7**	5 Where in the world is Barnaby Bear? **Chapters 8 and 9**
17 Global Eye **Chapter 10**	22 A contrasting locality overseas **Chapter 11**			

ideas page

Around the School 1

Background

The children are introduced to their local area. They are encouraged to locate houses using addresses, sequence buildings and landmarks on a journey to school and identify and label buildings in the High Street. The activity sheets should be used as starting points for work in your own locality, either through field visits or classwork. They might be enlarged and clipped to a flip-chart to rehearse each activity together before the children attempt it on their own. Resources such as large-scale local maps with photographs of local features stuck on will be useful.

Learning Objectives

- To locate places on a map, using addresses.
- To chart a simple route.
- To recognise physical and human features in the locality.
- To describe local features.

Mr Postman

Introducing and using the sheet
- Show the class a letter that has a clear local address. Talk about what each part of the address means, using maps of different scales to help.
- Look together at **Mr Postman** and help the children to join the letters to the correct addresses using a coloured crayon.
- Encourage the children to say what the addresses are for some of the other houses.

Follow-up/extension ideas
- Ask the children to bring in envelopes or cards that show their home address and help them to plot these on a local 1:1 250 Ordnance Survey map. Look at the map to find out who lives closest to and furthest away from school.
- Look at some of the addresses to which mail is sent or received by the school. Together, plot these on a map of the UK.
- Make displays of the addressed post and the plotted maps for both the school and the children's homes.

Journey to School

Introducing and using the sheet
- Help the children to describe Daniel's journey to school as shown on the plan (the directions will be in reverse to how they see the plan so turning the sheet upside-down may help). Encourage them to use language such as: 'First, he ... next, he ... finally, he ... .' Help them to give directions for other routes Daniel could take.
- Encourage two or three children in turn to describe their journey to school and each time a child identifies a landmark, note it on the board. Define 'landmark' ['easily recognised physical or human feature in the surroundings'] and discuss the importance of using landmarks to give and follow directions.
- Look together at the children's journeys on a large-scale map.

Follow-up/extension ideas
- The children could draw a 'memory map' of their journey to school (likely to be in picture form), showing the child's house, the school and the landmarks passed in between. Display these. Ask the children to describe their journey to a partner.
- **F** Take the class on a 'journey to school' for one of the children, helping them to take note of street names, house numbers, and other landmarks you pass.

Landmarks

Introducing and using the sheet
- This is a development of **Journey to School** that introduces the children to plan form. Explain what plan form is, how important it is on maps and show how simple 3D objects in the classroom look very different viewed in plan form.
- Using the sheet, help the children to describe the sequence of Lisa's journey to school in similar language to that used before.
- Some children might volunteer to describe their own journey home.

Follow-up/extension ideas
- Look at plan form in more detail. Give small groups of children a selection of 3D objects and ask them to draw the plan they can see. (Again, stress the difference between plan form and front view.)
- Take 36 photographs of different local landmarks. Bring them in and help individual children to sequence about six of them to show their journey to school.

Mr Postman

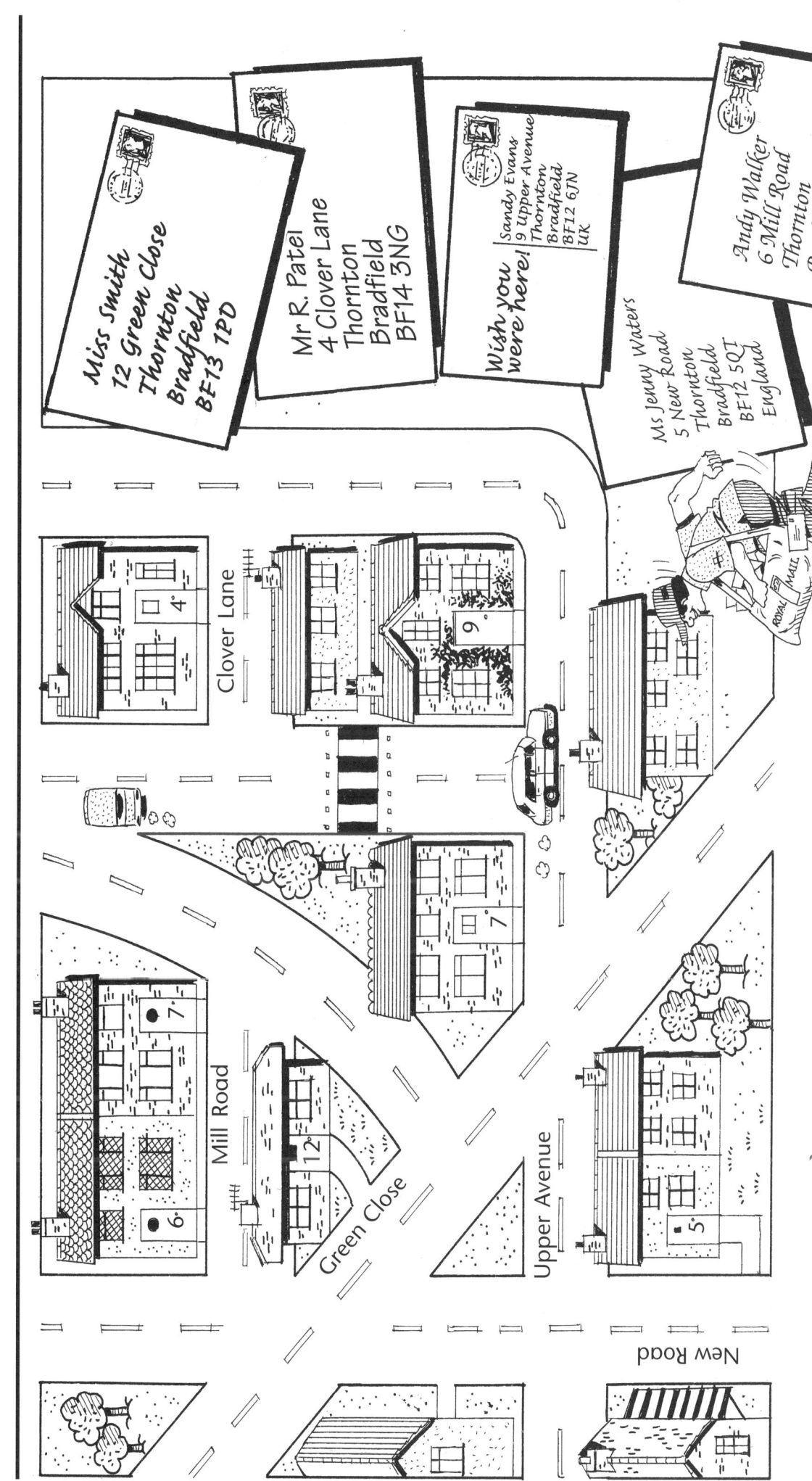

- Help the postman deliver his letters. Join each letter to the correct house.

Journey to School

- On a separate piece of paper, describe Daniel's journey to school. List the landmarks in the order he passes them.

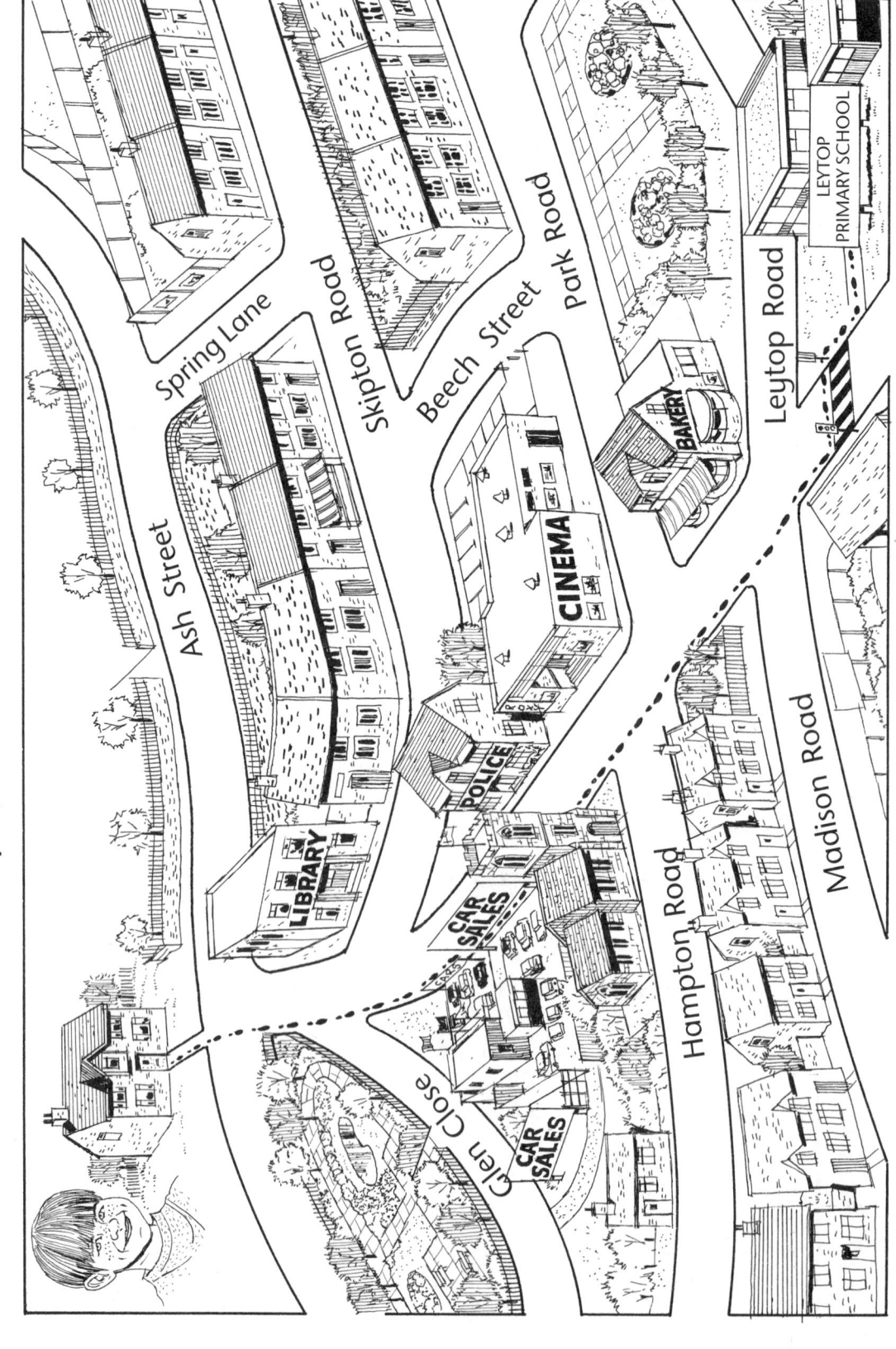

Landmarks

Number the buildings I pass in the correct order.

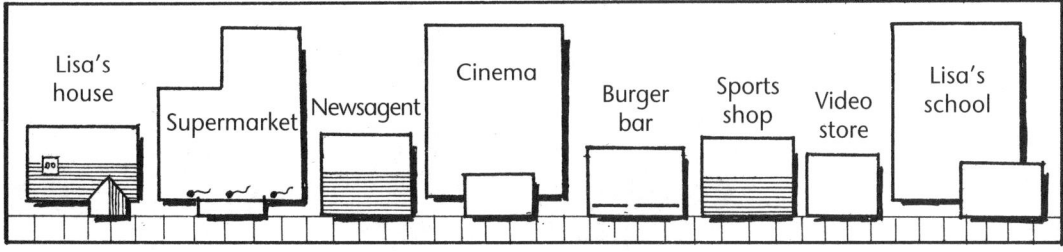

Victoria Street

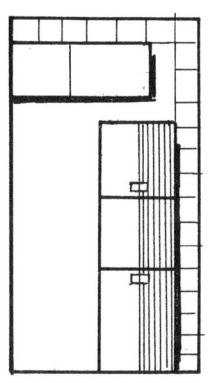 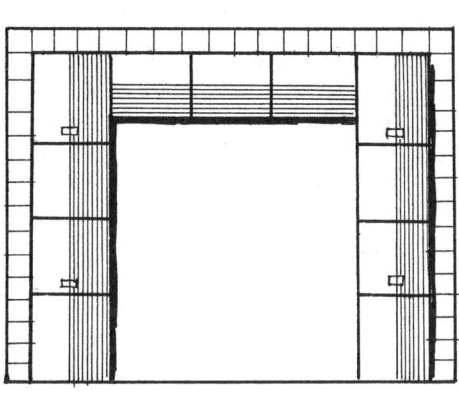 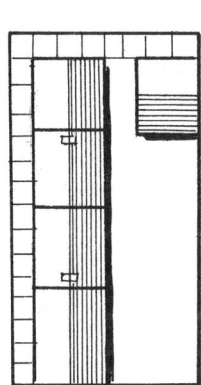

ideas page

Around the School 2

Background

These activity sheets extend children's thinking and understanding of a local environment. **Shop 'Til You Drop** looks at local shops and the different things they sell. **Nice and Nasty** encourages the children to think about the quality of a local environment and suggest how places could be improved. **Rob the Builder** shows how a house is built and asks the children to sequence its construction.

Learning Objectives

- To describe how places change over time.
- To express views on how appealing different features are.
- To identify building functions and uses.

Shop 'Til You Drop

Introducing and using the sheet

- Discuss with the children the different shops near school. Encourage them to say what kinds of things each shop might display in its window.
- Look together at the activity sheet focusing on what is being sold in some of the shops. Talk to the children about how to complete the sheet. Encourage them to say what each shop sells, then help them either to link each label to the correct shop or to write the correct name on each sign.

Follow-up/extension ideas

- Take photographs of shops in your local High Street. Help the children to make a frieze out of them and, in pairs, to add lists of what can be seen in each shop window.
- Set up in the classroom some mock shops, basing them as closely as possible on the local shops. Ask shopkeepers for spare advertising material to decorate your shops. Encourage the children to act out role-plays between shopkeepers and customers.

Nice and Nasty

Introducing and using the sheet

- Bring in photographs of 'nice' and 'nasty' places close to the school. Encourage the children to describe the photographs in groups, saying specifically what they like or dislike about each place.
- Introduce the activity sheet. Look at the first snapshot together and collect one-word descriptions that could be put in the box (for example: dark, noisy, smelly, dirty; or quiet, beautiful, safe, clean). Write these on a flip-chart. The children should put a tick or a cross next to the snapshot depending on whether or not they like the view.

Follow-up/extension ideas

- Help the children to locate the nice and nasty places in the photographs you brought in on a large-scale 1:1 250 map.
- Encourage the children to think about what makes a place nice or nasty and then, in groups, to make collections of 'nice' and 'nasty' words. Display these with the photographs and the map.

Rob the Builder

Introducing and using the sheet

- Encourage the children to think about the sequence of building a house, from the empty plot of land to the finished house with people moving in.
- Look together at the activity sheet. In small groups, the children should decide what the correct sequence is and reorder the sketches by numbering each one. They should then describe the changes that have occurred between each stage.

Follow-up/extension ideas

> ⚠ The children should be highly supervised during any visit to a building site.

- Bring in photographs of the building of a house nearby and help the children to sequence them.
- **F** Visit a building site and look in more detail at how houses are built. Mark the development on a local map.

Shop 'Til You Drop

- Write in the correct sign above each shop.

greengrocer	newsagent	fish 'n' chips	video store
shoe shop	toys	café	sports goods
computer games	clothes	grocer

- On a separate sheet, draw some shops yourself that you haven't labelled on the High Street.

Nice and Nasty

- If you think the snapshot is nice, put a green tick next to it. If nasty, put a red cross.
- Add a one-word description to say how each place is nice or nasty. Use the flip-chart of words you thought of together.

- Why do you think that some places are nice and others nasty?

Rob the Builder

Rob is building a house.

- Number the sketches from 1 to 6 and say what each change shows.

ideas page

How Can We Make Our Local Area Safer?

Background

These activity sheets investigate local traffic issues and tackle such problems as controlling traffic, parking and road safety. The children are encouraged to undertake a simple analysis of situations, ask questions and make decisions that will help them investigate and improve traffic movement. The sheets should be used to stimulate local work and so it would be useful to identify busy roads close to school that are sometimes congested. Simple traffic-survey recording sheets will be needed.

Learning Objectives

- To find out about the character of an area.
- To ask questions.
- To collect and analyse data.
- To make decisions about how to control traffic in an area.

Road Signs

Introducing and using the sheet

⚠ The children's safety is paramount near busy roads.

- Talk to the children about busy and quiet roads close to the school, the amount of traffic using them and where it is going.
- [F] Conduct a 15-minute traffic survey on a busy road close to school that is used by different kinds of traffic. Use a prepared traffic-survey tally chart showing cars, vans, lorries, buses and bicycles, having first discussed the categories with the children.
- Look at road signs, markings and other measures used to control and calm traffic. Point these out to the children, saying what they are and what effect they have. Take photographs to display in the classroom.
- Answers to sheet: 1 – no entry; 2 – no right turn; 3 – oncoming vehicles have priority; 4 – stop; 5 – pedestrian crossing; 6 – give way. NB The bus lane has no right turn so traffic can turn left out of the opposite street.

Follow-up/extension ideas

- Help the children to compare the amount and types of traffic and road signs in their survey street with those on the activity sheet.
- Make a class display of the most common road signs. The children should add captions after finding out the meanings.
- Invite in a visitor to talk about road safety.

Cartmel Street

Introducing and using the sheet

- Conduct an investigation into traffic numbers and types in a street near school at different times of day. At regular intervals, count the number of parked vehicles, note their registration numbers and make a note of the time.
- Look together at the activity sheet. Talk to the children about the amount and types of traffic found on Cartmel Street during the day.

Follow-up/extension ideas

- Ask further questions about the vehicles parked in Cartmel Street, for example: Who do you think would be using the vans at 10am? At what time were most vehicles parked? Where do you think the people go when they park their cars?
- Use simple graphing software to show the numbers of vehicles parked in Cartmel Street at different times of day.
- Repeat these suggestions using your local street.

Calming Traffic

Introducing and using the sheet

- Talk to the children about different ways of slowing down traffic. Explain each method and, where possible, use photographs to help them understand what the different calming measures are, what they look like and what they do.
- Look together at the map in the activity sheet, discussing what each traffic-calming measure means and the best places to put them. Encourage the children to plot them in plan form if they can. They should work in pairs.

Follow-up/extension ideas

- In a class discussion, encourage selected pairs of children to say where they placed each traffic-calming measure and why.
- From the playground, look at the road markings and signs around your own school and discuss what each is for.
- Hand out copies of an enlarged map of the school and its nearby streets. Help small groups of children to mark on some traffic-calming measures for making local roads safer.

Road Signs

Traffic signs are used to make our roads safer.
- Find out the meaning of each sign and write it in the box.

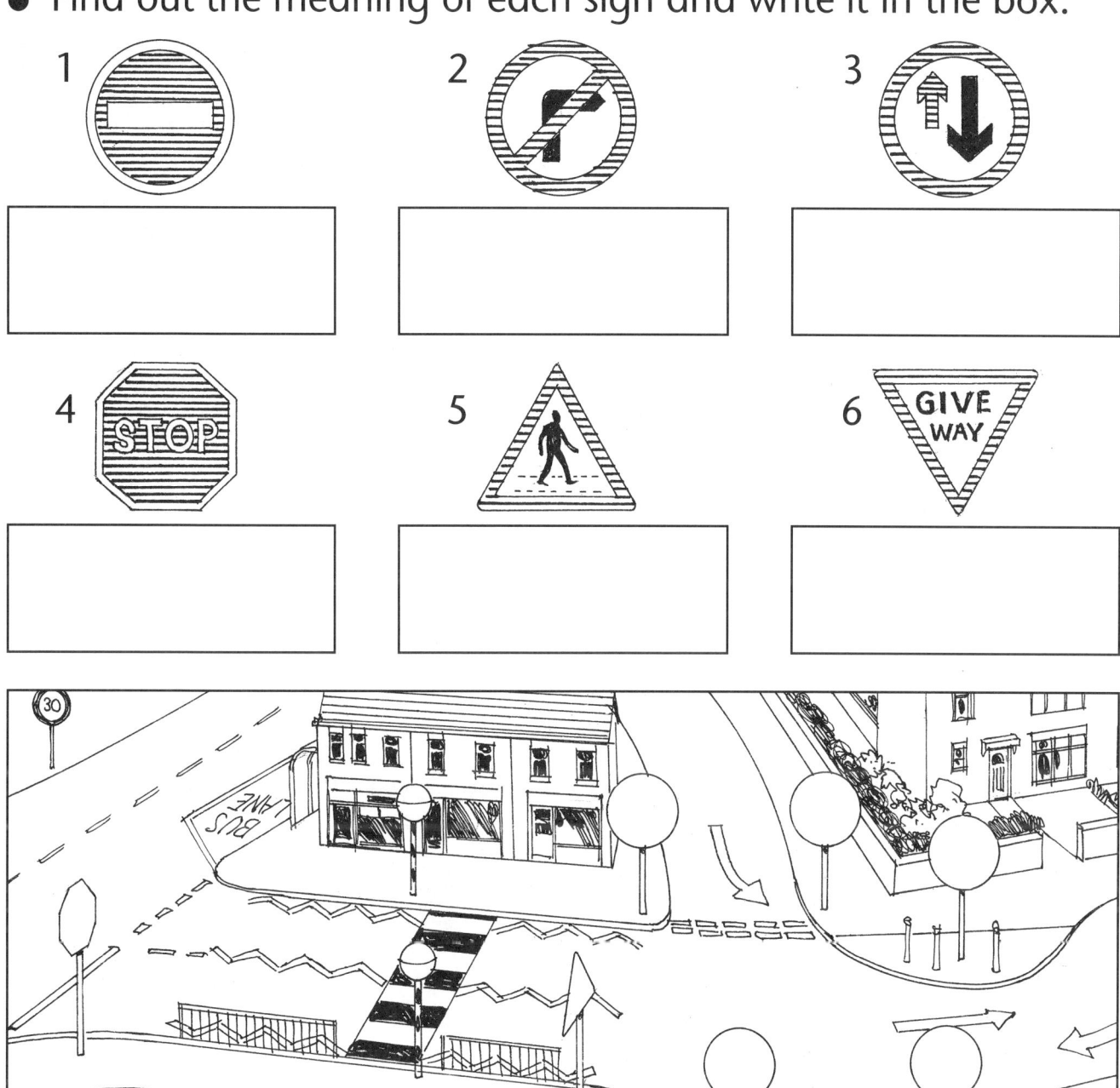

- Fill in each blank sign in the picture with the correct sign from above.

Cartmel Street

Time: 8am

Time: 10am

Time: 3pm

- How many vehicles are in Cartmel Street at:

  8am?

  10am?

  3pm?

- How many vehicles have been parked all day long?

- At what time were the most delivery and repair vehicles in Cartmel Street?

Calming Traffic

Make the area around North Street Primary School a safer place for children, parents and motorists.

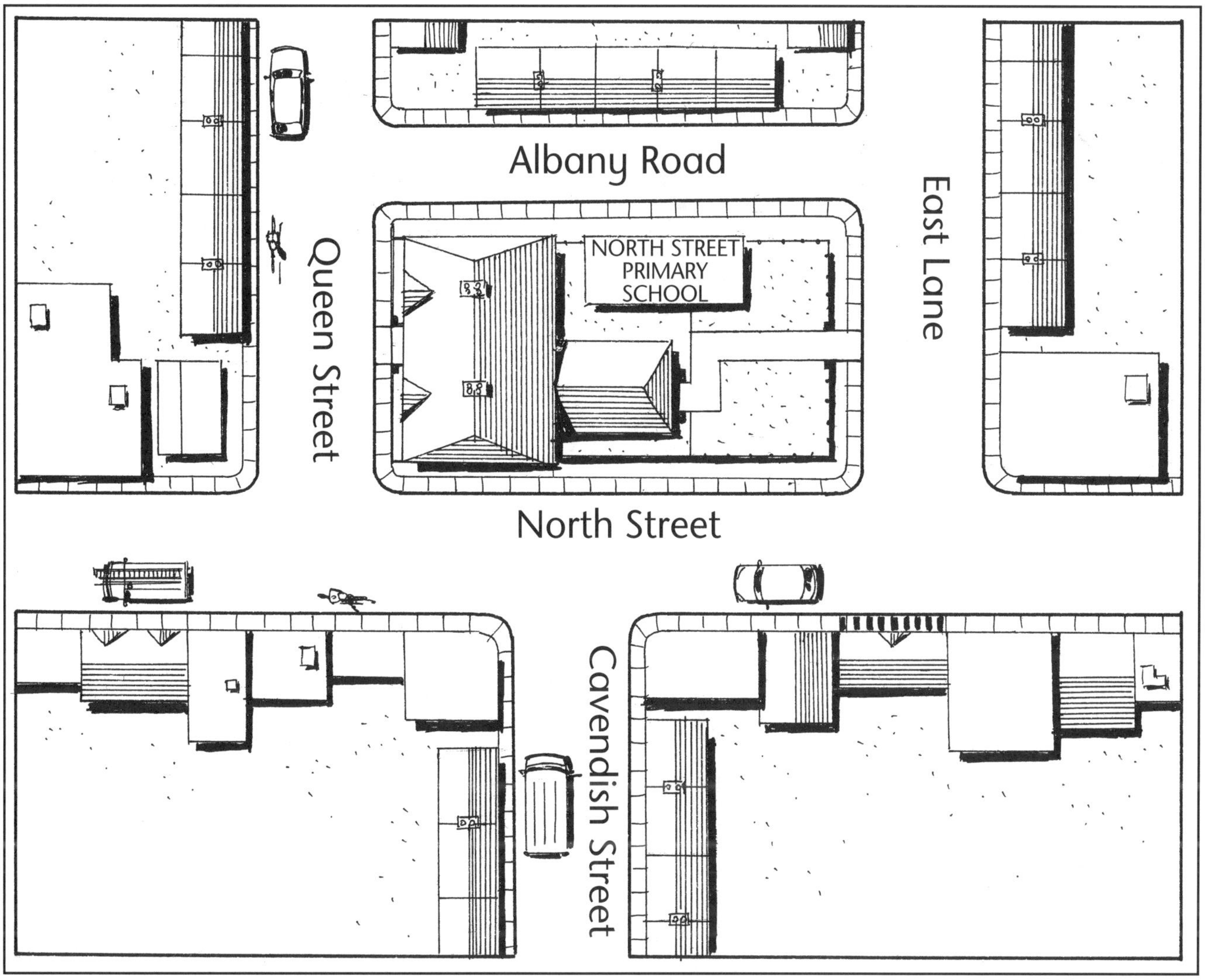
Albany Road
NORTH STREET PRIMARY SCHOOL
Queen Street
East Lane
North Street
Cavendish Street

- Draw in these features where you think they would help the most.

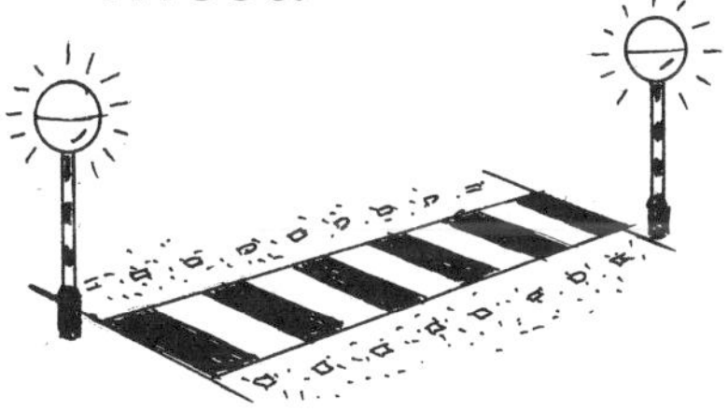

zebra crossing

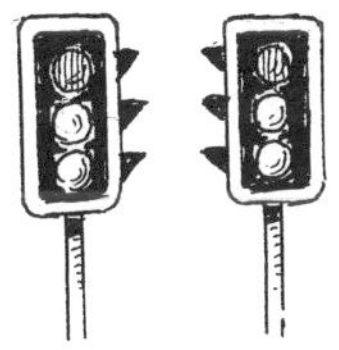

traffic lights

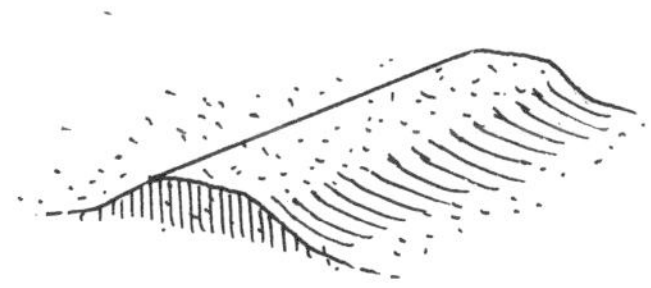

sleeping policemen

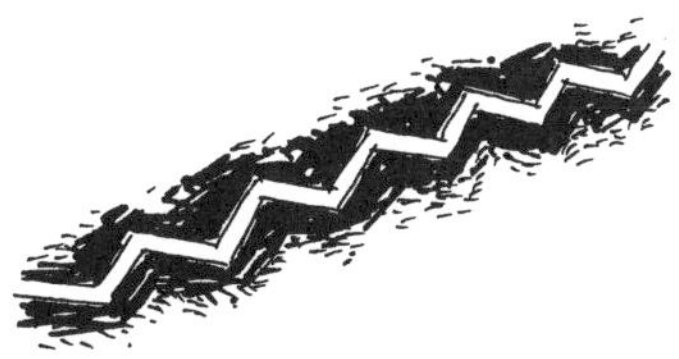

zig-zag yellow lines

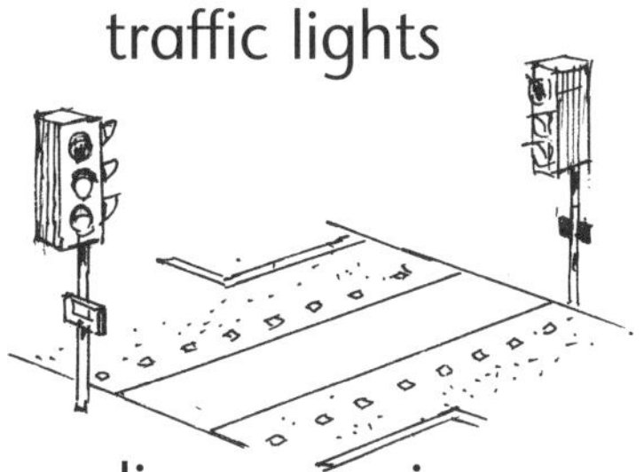

pelican crossing

double yellow lines

ideas page

An Island Home 1

Background

This unit develops the children's understanding of places by investigating a fictitious island. Throughout the unit, the children are given the opportunity to look at physical and human features, settlement, transport and the lives and work of the islanders, and to compare the island with their own local environment. They are encouraged to express views about the island and the people who live there, so helping to develop their literacy skills.

Learning Objectives

- To notice the physical and human features of a place.
- To use a key and understand symbols.
- To identify different forms of transport.
- To compare a fictitious environment with a familiar one.

Summer Isle

Introducing and using the sheet
- Talk about the different physical and human features on the island. Encourage the children to understand what each feature is and what it looks like.
- In front of the class, put the different features into two columns, one for physical and one for human features. Discuss the activity sheet. The children could point to the correct word for each feature on the map or write it in.

Follow-up/extension ideas
- Help the children to compose lists of words that describe each of the features (e.g. for beach: sandy; rough).
- Encourage pairs of children to invent their own island. They should draw a map of it, including some of the features shown on Summer Isle. Ask them to give their island a name.

What is Summer Isle Like?

Introducing and using the sheet
- Talk to the children about 'symbols' – what they are, how they are used and why. Look at the symbols used on an Ordnance Survey map.
- Look at the symbols used in the key on the sheet. Ask the children what they think each represents and where the best place for it is on the map (they may need to refer to the map on page 17). They should then draw these in (decide with them how many examples of each to include).

Follow-up/extension ideas
- Discuss where on the map the children put the symbols and why.
- Encourage the children to describe the physical and human features of Summer Isle.
- Ask the children to imagine they are on Summer Isle. Where would they go if they wanted to shop? Where could they make sand-castles or play on the beach? Where would they go for a walk to the lighthouse? Where do they think roads are needed?
- The children might add some of these features to their own island.

Getting Around

Introducing and using the sheet
- Talk about the ways of getting around your local area and list them on a flip-chart.
- Look together at the key on the activity sheet and discuss the types of transport used on the island. Help the children to identify a bridleway (a track for horses), a road for cars, and a path for walkers only.
- Look again at the physical features of the island and discuss how these will affect transport links. For example, bridges will be needed so that the road can cross water.

Follow-up/extension ideas
- Ask the children whether they think it is difficult to get around the island or not. Discuss how transport links around the island are different from those around the school.
- Use the plans from *Folens Geography Big Book* (F4538) to show how roads cross railways, rivers and so on.

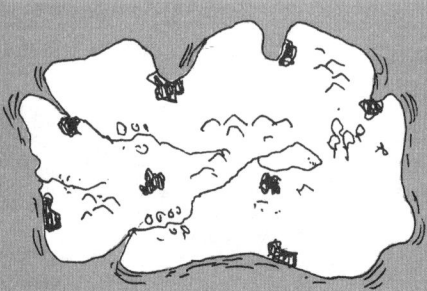

16

Summer Isle

- Look carefully at the map and label each feature. Choose from the word-bank.

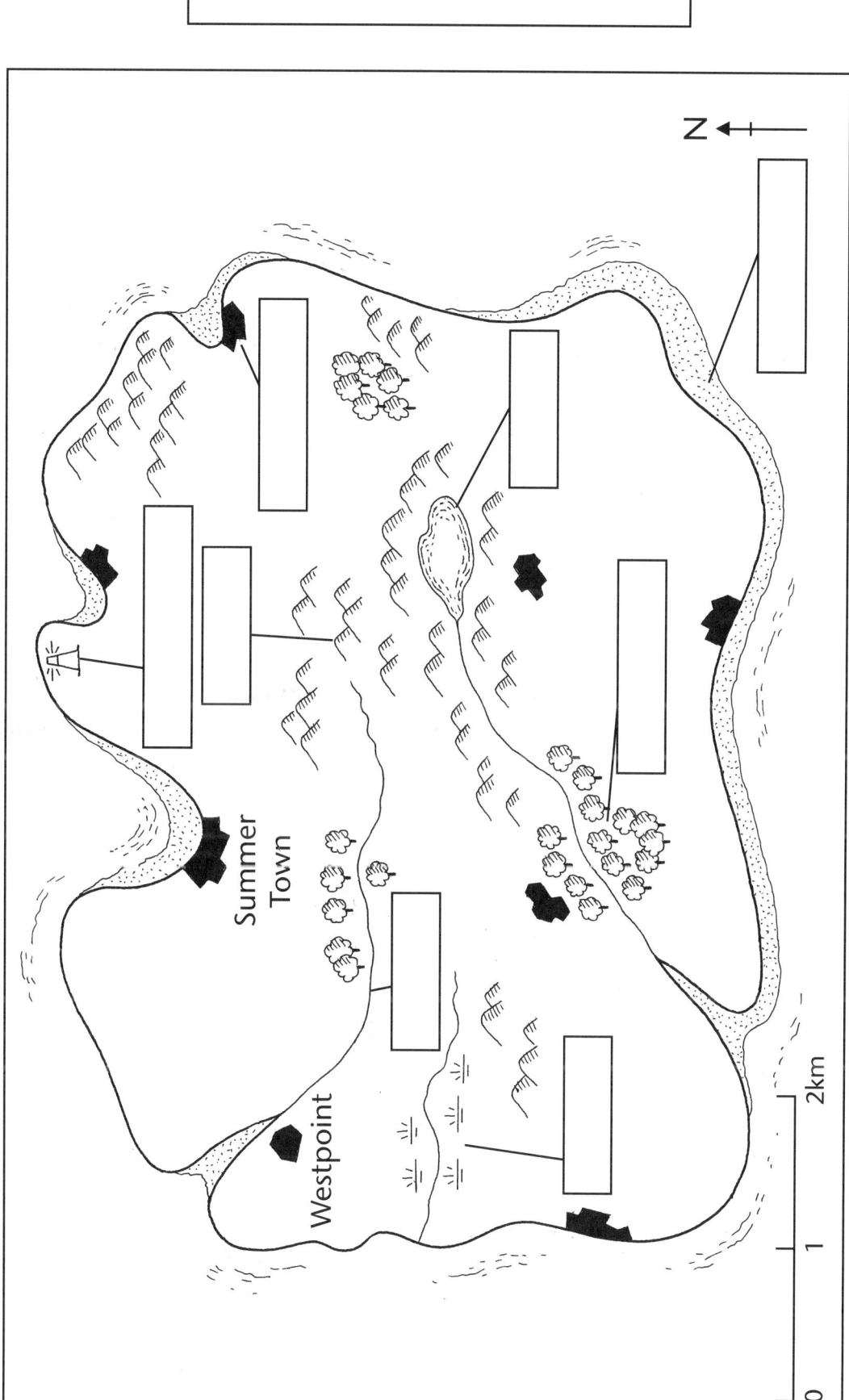

hills
lighthouse
beach
marsh
lake
stream
woodland
settlement

What is Summer Isle Like?

- Work out what each symbol means and write it in the key.

Key

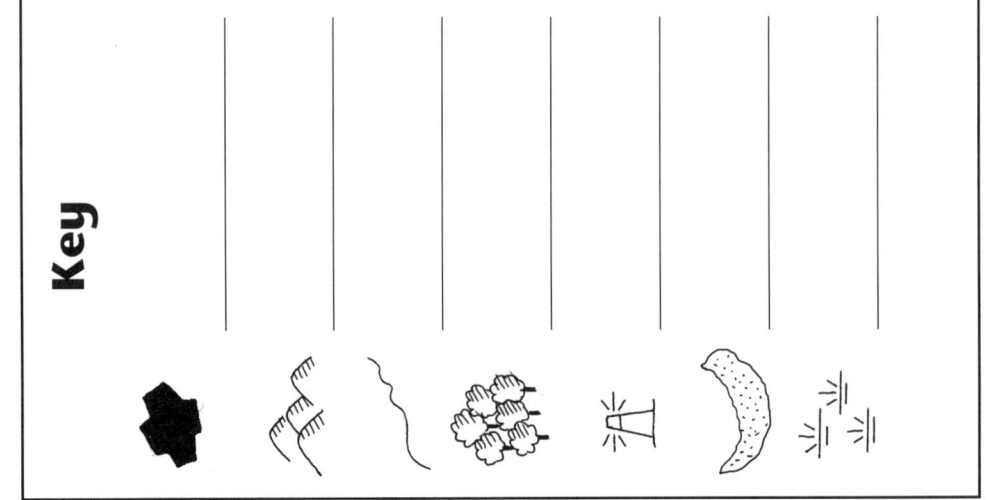

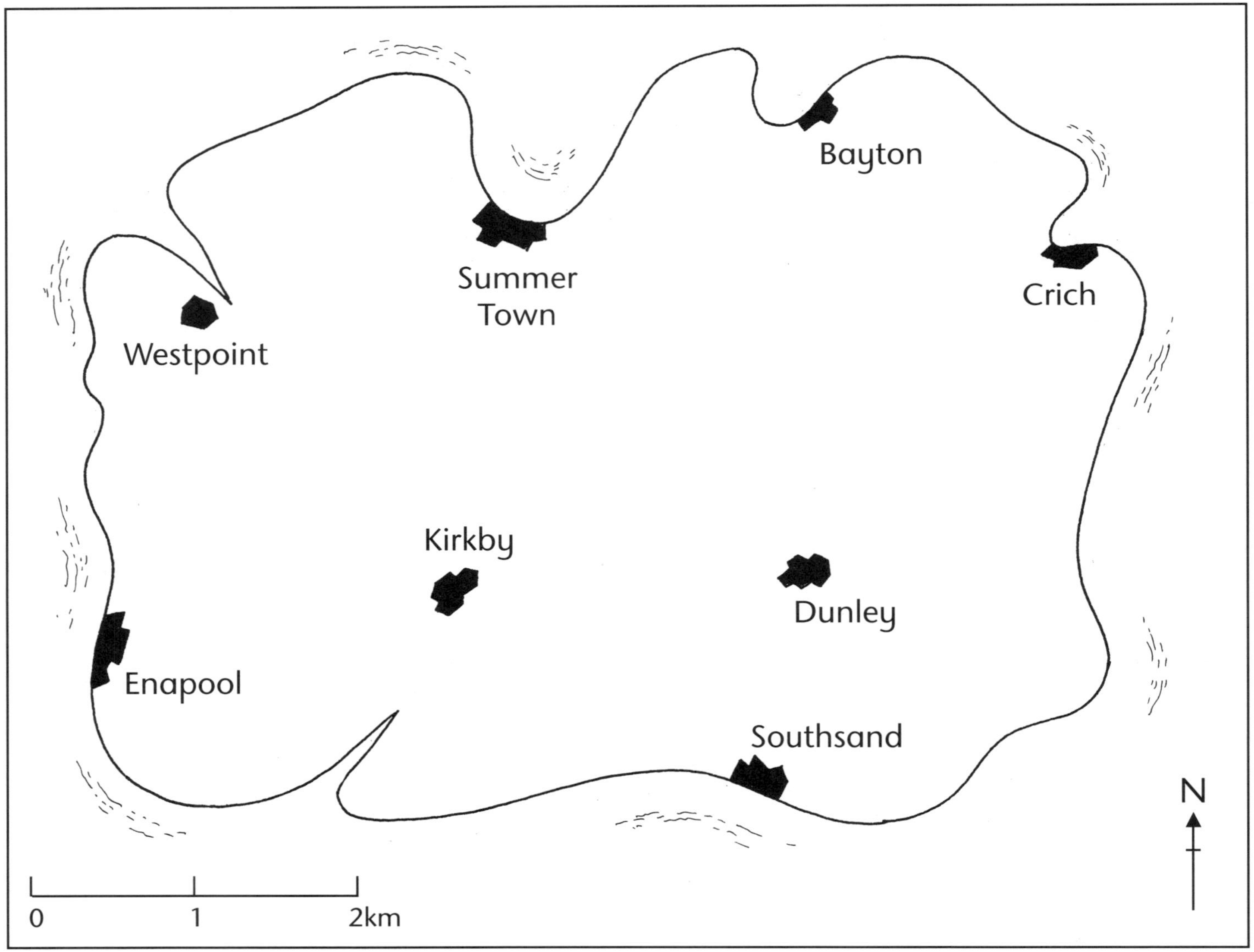

- Use the symbols to mark in what you feel Summer Isle is like.

Getting Around

Show how people get around Summer Isle.

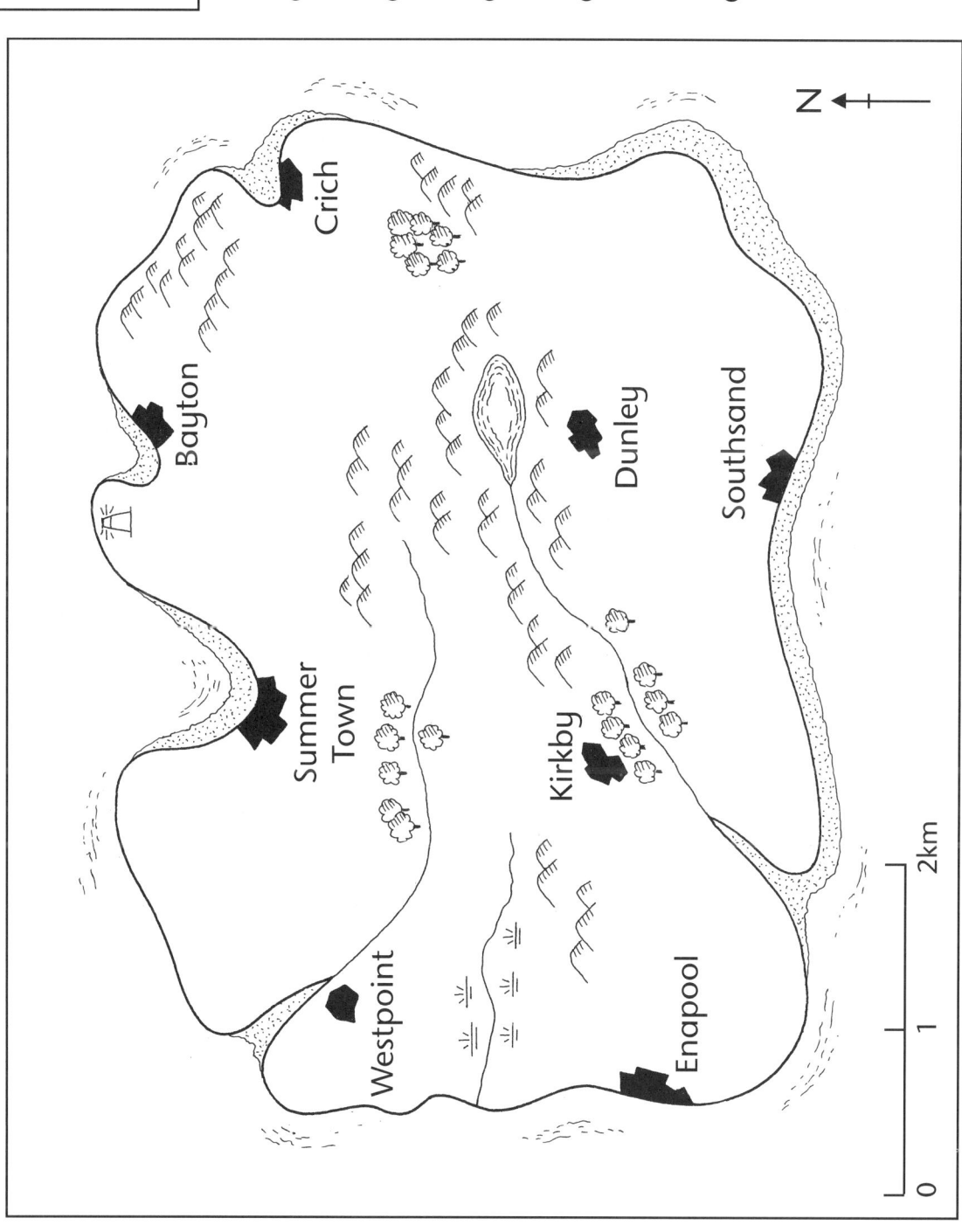

Key

= road -- bridleway
= track --- footpath

- Draw a road from Summer Town to Enapool.
- Draw a track from Kirkby to Dunley.
- Draw a bridleway from Westpoint to Enapool.
- Draw a footpath from Southsand to Bayton. Try to keep close to the coast.
- Draw in two more routes. Look out for hills, lakes and streams – avoid these if you can.

ideas page

An Island Home 2

Background

Job Finder looks at the often multiple jobs that people do on a small island and stimulates discussion about how islanders organise their working day and year to reflect the changing seasons and patterns of tourism. **Panorama** encourages the children to compare Summer Isle with their own locality and to identify features of each. **Greetings from Summer Isle** asks the children to describe life on the island and to consider the advantages and disadvantages of living on a small island.

Learning Objectives

- To notice the physical and human features of a place.
- To use a key and understand symbols.
- To identify different forms of transport.
- To compare a fictitious environment with a familiar one.
- To express likes and dislikes about a place.

Job Finder

Introducing and using the sheet
- Talk to the children about the jobs people might do on the island and the places they would work; for example, a farmer would work in a 'croft'. Questions about the children's own holidays might help stimulate thought: How many people work in a hotel or café? What kinds of shops are there? Who fills the cars with petrol and mends them? Look at the types of job shown on the sheet.
- Explain that many islanders have a number of jobs so that they can earn a reasonable income.

Follow-up/extension ideas
- Copy the activity sheet onto card, cut out each figure and fold back the tabs to stand them up. They can be placed on a map of Summer Isle to show where each job is done.
- Encourage the children to make a short play based on the Summer Isle characters, or set up role-play areas of the places in which different jobs are done and help them to act out activities in the workplace.

Panorama

Introducing and using the sheet
- An A3 copy of the cards should be cut out for the children in advance of the lesson.
- Talk about the landscape, coastline and settlements on the island.
- Help the children to put their cards together, like a jigsaw, to make a panorama of Summer Isle. They should use the map on page 17 as a guide.

Follow-up/extension ideas
- From a vantage point, take a panorama of photographs of the locality around the school, or obtain an aerial photograph, and bring these into class.
- Mount a set of cards showing the panorama of Summer Isle and write accompanying labels describing physical and human features. After a class discussion, help individual children to attach labels to the panorama. Then do the same for the local photographs. Encourage the children to identify similarities and differences between the two places under headings such as 'Houses' and 'Landscape'.

Greetings from Summer Isle

Introducing and using the sheet
- Discuss with the children what it would be like to live on the island. Encourage them to list what things they would miss and what things they would be able to do on the island that they cannot do in their local area. Ask them whether or not they would like to live on Summer Isle.
- Help the children to complete the postcard from Summer Isle, adding their family name and address as well as a message. Discuss the kinds of things they might include in their message. Model some ideas on a flip-chart, giving the children some sentence starters before they move off to complete the sheet.

Follow-up/extension ideas
- Encourage the children to use some of the activity sheets in this unit to describe a journey around the island. Some children could do this in the form of picture postcards with sketches and visitor information.

Job Finder

Find the correct job for each of the islanders.
- On each person's tab, write in the job that he or she does. Choose from the list below.

| mechanic | fisherman | postman |
| shopkeeper | captain | taxi driver | farmer |

Panorama

- Put together these mixed-up cards in the correct order to show a panorama of Summer Isle.

Greetings from Summer Isle

- Imagine that you are on holiday in Summer Isle.
- Send a postcard home. Say what the island is like and what you have done during your stay.
- Remember to fill in the name and address.

ideas page

Going to the Seaside 1

Background

The seaside is explored during this unit, which follows Tom and his family through their planning and taking of one holiday and their preparation for the next. The activity sheets look at the kinds of holiday it is possible to take, the different features that particular holiday resorts offer and at the family exploring their chosen resort. Much of the work draws from and extends the children's existing knowledge and experiences of holiday resorts. Parents are required to help in the completion of **Tom's Holiday Hunt**.

Learning Objectives

- To use secondary sources.
- To identify the main features of a seaside resort.
- To compare localities.
- To develop an awareness of the wider world.

Last Year's Holiday

Introducing and using the sheet
- Talk to the children about the kinds of holiday it is possible to have in the UK: by the sea; in the countryside; in a town or city; or at a special attraction such as a theme park or stately home.
- Encourage the children to remember where they have been on holiday and make a list on a flip-chart (include day-trips).
- With the children, put these into one of four categories: seaside; countryside; town or city; special attraction.
- Look together at the activity sheet and help the children to put each destination into one of the four categories.

Follow-up/extension ideas
- Prepare a simple map of the UK, showing all of the places in the sheet marked with dots. Hand around atlases and help the children, either individually or in pairs, to name the places marked.
- Draw a simple bar chart showing 2C's holiday details, or enter them into a database.
- Conduct a similar exercise using the holiday details supplied by your class.

Tom's Holiday Hunt

Introducing and using the sheet
- Locate the most popular seaside resorts on a UK map. Identify those the children have visited. Ask them what they did and saw at these resorts. Did they bring home any postcards or souvenirs? Add the resort most popular with the class at the top of the notepad in the sheet, before copying for the children.
- After discussion, the sheet should be completed as homework. The children should ask at home for information about the resorts on the map and then describe them on the notepad. As preparation, help them compose some notes about the resorts they know. For example: Blackpool – 'It has a tower and a funfair' is sufficient.

Follow-up/extension ideas
- Put each resort name on the top of a piece of A3 paper. Use the information the children have collected to write more detailed notes about each. Focus on the resorts the children have visited.
- Add pictures of each resort from brochures and display around the UK map.
- Help the children to find out, using atlases, which resort is closest to the school and which is furthest away. They could work out the distances and how long each journey would take in a car travelling at 60km per hour.

Viewpoint

Introducing and using the sheet
- Bring in some local information, tourist picture maps and maps of town centres that show actual buildings rather than just street layouts. Encourage the children to find specific places.
- Now look at the activity sheet. Single out features and help the children to locate them in the view and on the map and then to label the map.

Follow-up/extension ideas
- Talk about the main features of a seaside resort. Look at how the land is used and compare with local uses. Why do the children think seaside resorts are often long and thin? [Because everything crowds along the seafront.]
- Help the children to label tourist maps of your nearest seaside resort and of your local town and display these.

Last Year's Holiday

- Look at some of the places the children in 2C have been on holiday.

- Use a map or an atlas to say whether these places are by the sea or in the countryside, are towns or cities, or are special attractions such as theme parks.

Tom's Holiday Hunt

- Find out about the resorts on the map.

- Write a brief description of each resort in the notebook.

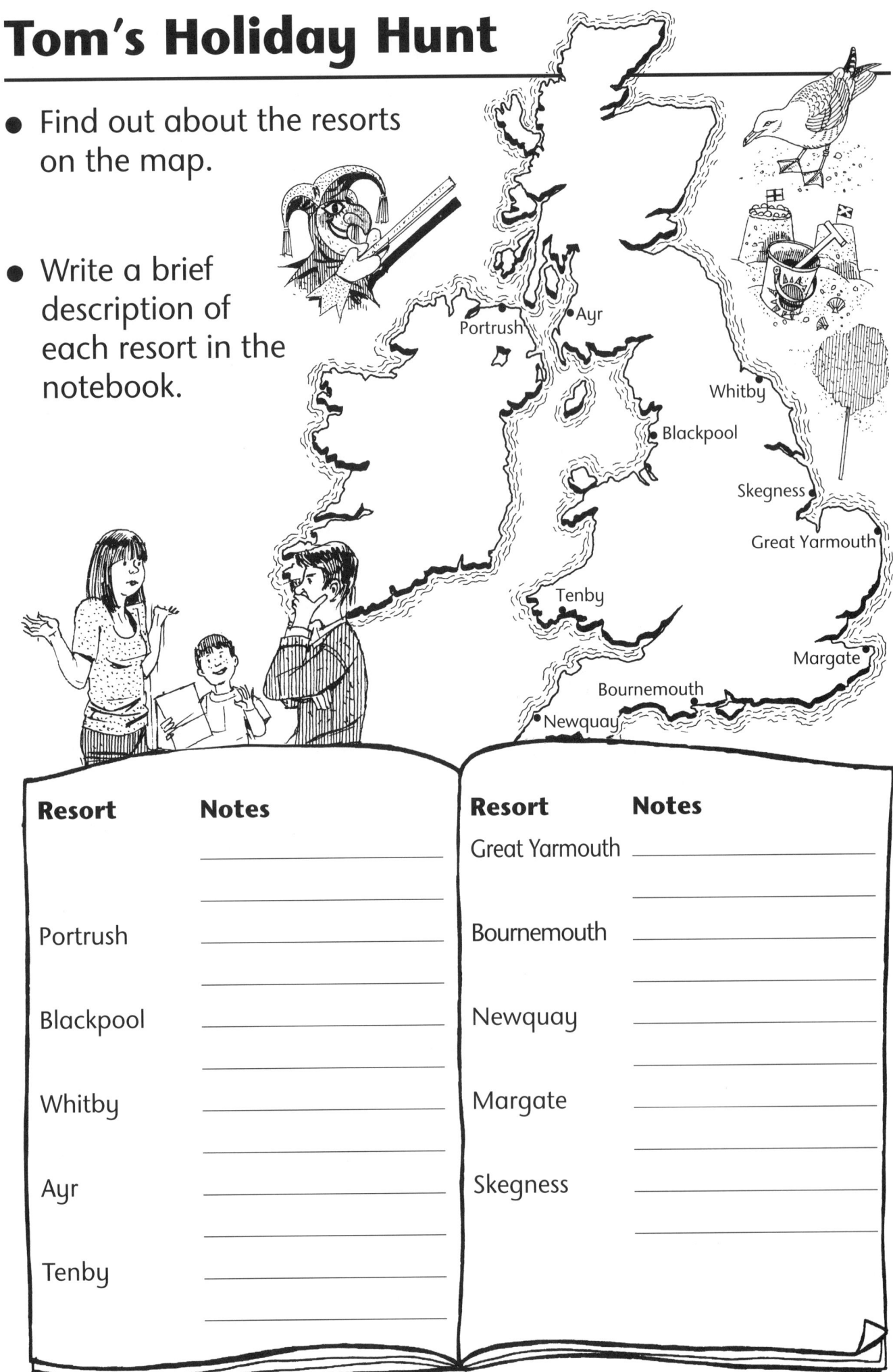

Resort	Notes	Resort	Notes
		Great Yarmouth	
Portrush		Bournemouth	
Blackpool		Newquay	
Whitby		Margate	
Ayr		Skegness	
Tenby			

Viewpoint

1. beach
2. pier
3. sea
4. funfair
5. monument
6. castle
7. promenade
8. shops

- On the map of Weston-on-Sea, number the features that you can see in the view. The first one has been done for you.

ideas page

Going to the Seaside 2

Background

These activity sheets develop the themes introduced in the previous unit. **Looking at Buildings** continues the exploration of the differences in uses of land and buildings between a seaside resort and an inland urban locality. **Didn't We Have a Lovely Time!** considers, through a series of 'Victorian' snapshots, how resorts have changed over time. **Faraway Shores** adds a global dimension, with Tom and his family, in the winter, thinking about a more distant holiday for the following summer.

Learning Objectives

- To use secondary sources.
- To identify the main features of a seaside resort.
- To compare localities.
- To understand how places change over time.
- To develop an awareness of the wider world.

Looking at Buildings

Introducing and using the sheet
- Talk about the different ways that buildings in a town are used. On a flip-chart, give examples of various uses, such as chemists, shoe shops and banks.
- Look together at the activity sheet and talk about the different ways that buildings are used in a seaside resort. Discuss the things that shops in a seaside resort sell, or the functions other buildings perform.

Follow-up/extension ideas
- Encourage the children to draw some buildings likely to be found in the local High Street. Make a frieze out of their drawings. Label each building, giving its name and saying what it sells.
- Help the children to identify how and why land use and building use differs between seaside and inland towns. To stimulate thought, ask them questions such as: What do people like to do when they are on holiday? Why don't we find these shops in our own High Street [if inland]?

Didn't We Have a Lovely Time!

Introducing and using the sheet
- Show the children some photographs taken long ago, preferably of places they know. Ask small groups to note the differences in clothes, buildings and transport between then and now. Encourage the groups in turn to say what they have noticed about each aspect and jot down the most important differences on a flip-chart.
- Introduce the activity sheet. In pairs the children should look again for differences in clothes, buildings and transport and the general character of the seaside between Victorian times and the present day. Add any extra information they find to the flip-chart.

Follow-up/extension ideas
- Help the children to make a display of pictures and photographs of a seaside resort from Victorian times next to similar ones from the present day. Use reference books and brochures and on-line sources to help.

Faraway Shores

Introducing and using the sheet
- Ask the children about the places abroad that they have been to, on holiday or to visit family.
- Map the places that the children have visited. Make a collection of photographs and old postcards, especially those from seaside resorts, and add them to the display.
- Look together at the activity sheet. Talk about each of the places on Tom's suitcase and the map. Use atlases to help the children locate each place.

Follow-up/extension ideas
- Collect posters from travel agents and tourist information offices showing seaside resorts in different parts of the world.
- Give small groups of children a selection of brochures. Help each group to find 6–8 seaside resorts around the world. Encourage them to say what they like about the pictures and decide which resorts they would like to visit and why.

Looking at Buildings

Buildings are used in different ways in seaside resorts and inland towns.
- See how the buildings are used in the seaside resort of Weston-on-Sea.

- Fill in the signs and windows in Tom's Town to show how buildings in towns are used.

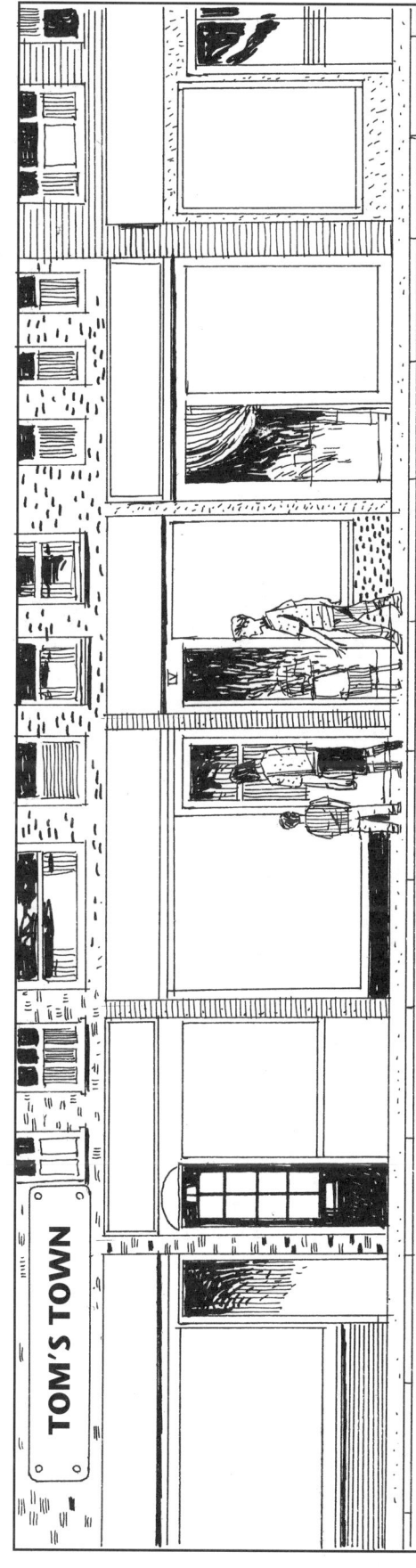

Didn't We Have a Lovely Time!

- Look carefully at the photographs above and those supplied by your teacher.
- Talk about how the clothes, transport, buildings and beaches were different in Victorian times from how they are today.

Faraway Shores

The World

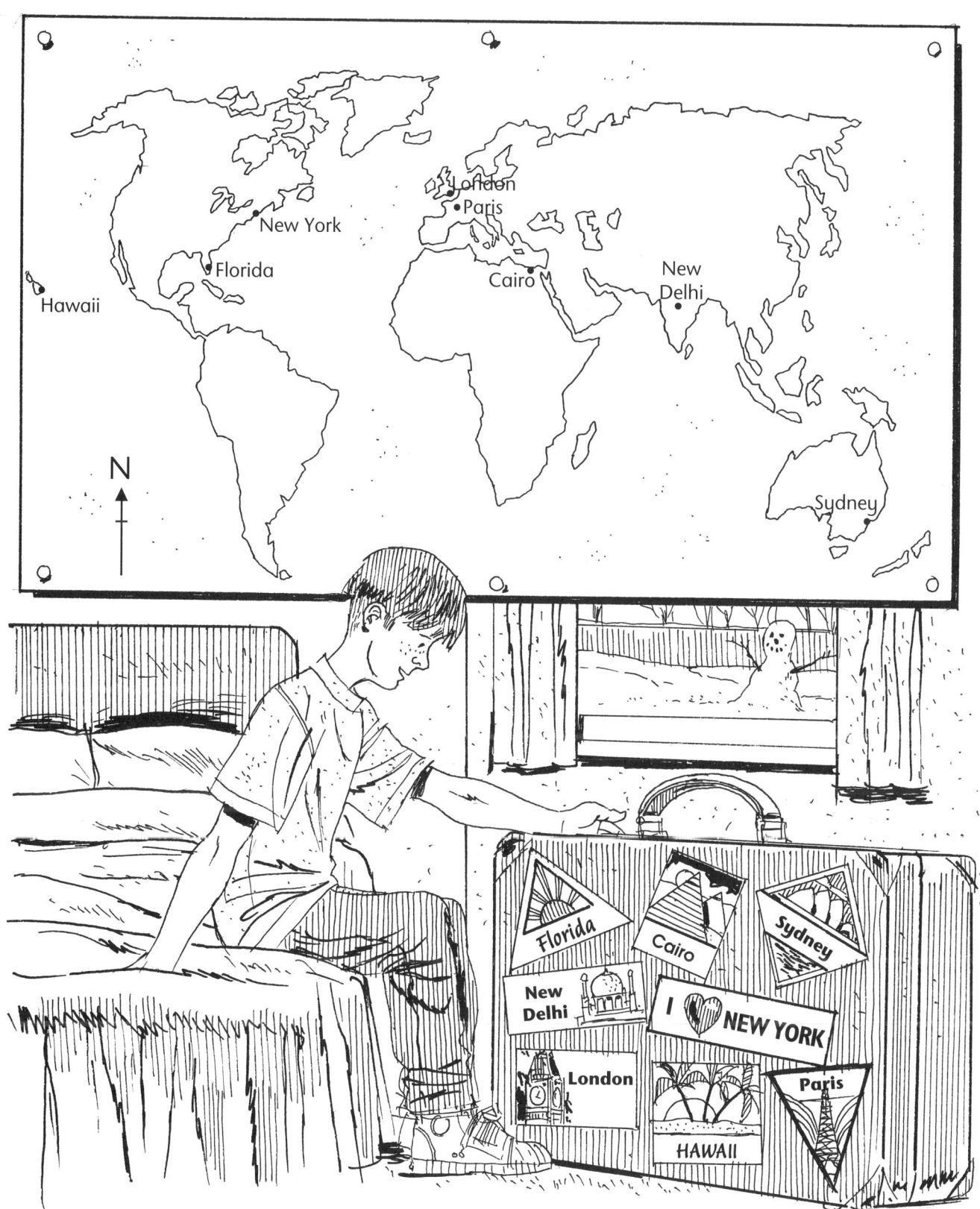

- Look at the stickers on Tom's old suitcase.
- Use an atlas to find out in which country each place on Tom's map is.

ideas page

Where in the World is Gordon the Gnome?

Background

The QCA material that this unit and the next are based on looks at the travels of Barnaby Bear. These two units use a new character, Gordon the Gnome. The units should be visited at intervals throughout years 1 and 2. They introduce the children to places in the wider world, including their climate, landscape, culture and human activities, as well as what to pack and how to travel to different destinations. To maximise interest, encourage colleagues to take Gordon on holiday with them and to photograph him in different situations (a good supply of plastic gnomes will be useful!).

Learning Objectives

- To locate places on maps and in atlases.
- To describe the characteristics of places.
- To become aware of the differences between places.
- To identify the types of transport used to make journeys.

Gordon the Gnome

Introducing and using the sheet
- Encourage the children to name the different kinds of transport they would use if they were travelling to a holiday destination quite close and again to one far away.
- Look together at the activity sheet and help the children to identify each form of transport shown. Ask them to find Gordon in each picture.

Follow-up/extension ideas
- Find out from the children what transport they used to travel to the last resort they went to on holiday. Use the information collected to draw a graph on a flip-chart. Then help the children to draw a similar graph of their own.

Globetrotter

Introducing and using the sheet
- Talk about the different kinds of holidays that people have, for example beach holidays, skiing and adventure holidays. Encourage the children to name the kinds of holidays that they have been on.
- Look together at the activity sheet and explain the terms used in the word-bank. Help the children to label each kind of holiday shown and find Gordon.

Follow-up/extension ideas
- Split the children into groups and ask each to make a collage of a different type of holiday, using information and pictures from brochures. Make a display by sticking the collages around a world map and linking each to a place on the map where the holiday is likely to occur.

Get Packing

Introducing and using the sheet
Get Packing closely relates to the previous activity, **Globetrotter**.
- Talk about each of the items in the wardrobe and help the children to label them. Ask them what kind of holiday each item would be packed for.
- Ask pairs of children to choose a holiday destination for Gordon from those on the sheet and to write it on the suitcase label. They should then pack for him by writing the name of each item in the suitcase or joining it with a line to the suitcase.

Follow-up/extension ideas
- Encourage the pairs to say what they have chosen to pack for Gordon and why.
- Bring a suitcase into class and together pack it with items that Gordon may need for a beach holiday in the Mediterranean (as an alternative the children could draw the items and put the drawings into a shoe-box suitcase). This could be repeated for a range of different destinations and displayed with Gordon.

Gordon the Gnome

- Can you find Gordon the Gnome?
- Fill in each label to say what kind of transport he is travelling on.

Globetrotter

- Label each snapshot with the kind of holiday it shows (choose from the word-bank).

city break
beach holiday
skiing
activity holiday

Get Packing

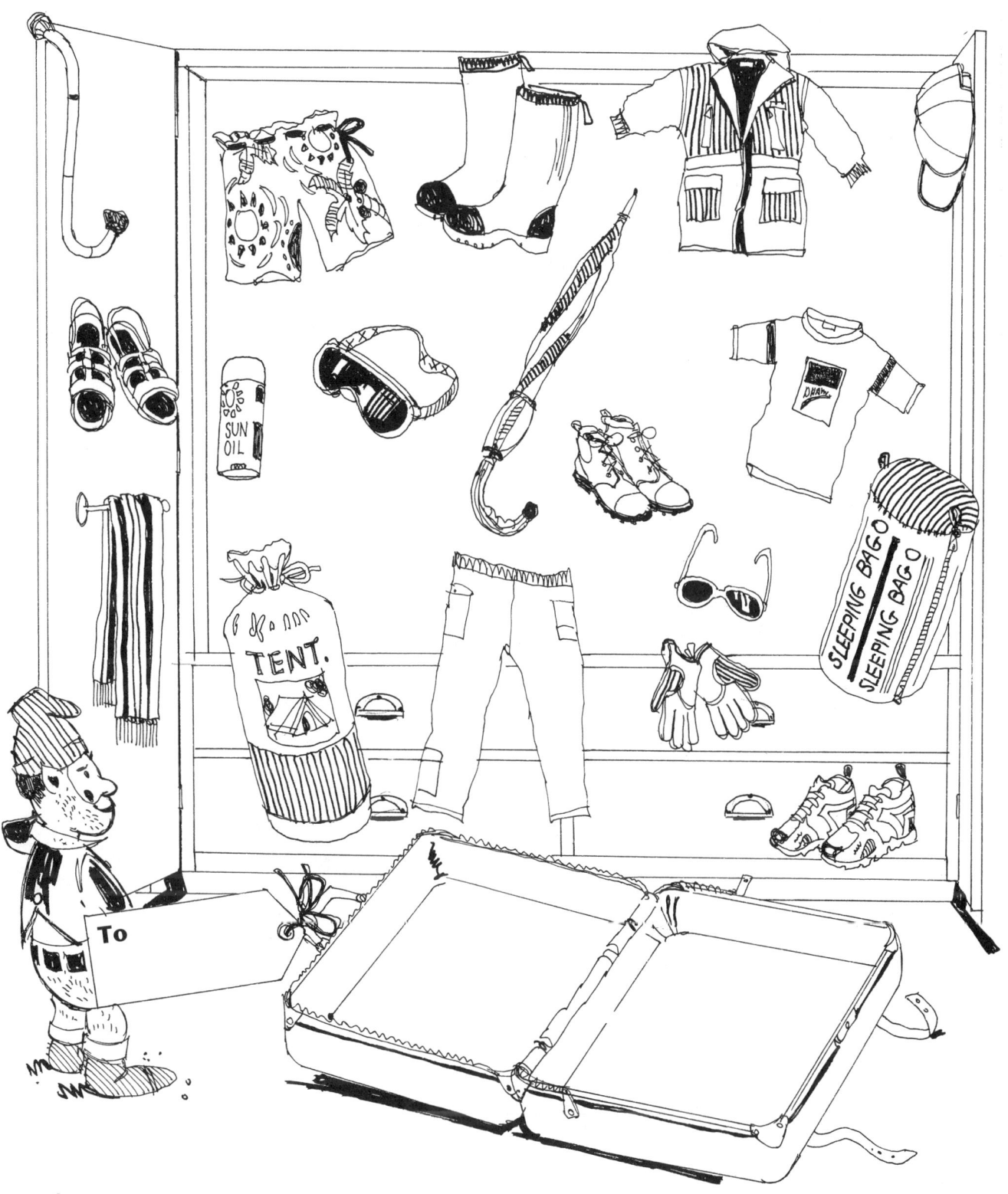

- Label the suitcase with a holiday destination for Gordon.
- Pack Gordon's suitcase with the items you think he'll need by linking the items to the case or writing their names in it.

ideas page — Where in the World are You?

Background

The holiday theme from the previous unit is continued in this one, which goes on to explore the weather in different holiday resorts, the artefacts that tell us about the character of a resort, and how we travel to different destinations.

Learning Objectives

- To locate places on maps and in atlases.
- To describe the characteristics of places.
- To become aware of the differences between places.
- To identify the types of transport used to make journeys.
- To understand that different places experience different weather conditions.

Weather Report

Introducing and using the sheet
- Talk to the children about holiday postcards: what they are, why people send them and the kinds of information they contain.
- Show the children some postcards. Talk about the picture on the front and read out and discuss the message on the back.
- Look together at the activity sheet. Read the messages on the postcards in turn, concentrating on the weather information. Introduce the children to the Met Office weather symbol (shown in more detail on page 48). Explain each symbol.
- Encourage pairs of children to describe the weather each holiday resort is receiving. They should draw the appropriate weather symbol next to each picture to represent the weather being experienced.

Follow-up/extension ideas
- Ask the children to write a mock postcard to Gordon from a resort they have recently been to. They should describe the weather they experienced there.

Souvenir

Introducing and using the sheet
- If possible, show the children artefacts or souvenirs collected from another country (several members of staff could bring back odd items from their holidays at resorts in the UK and abroad). Talk about the items collected.
- Look together at the activity sheet and talk about the collections of artefacts shown in each collage. Encourage the children to identify the place from which each collection originated. They should also try to find Gordon in each.

Follow-up/extension ideas
- Put the children in groups and allocate each group a different country (for which you have a collection of artefacts). Distribute the relevant artefacts to the groups ask them each to make a collage out of the artefacts and posters and maps from their country. Display the collages along with selected holiday photographs. (Some artefacts may be photocopied so that originals can be reused.)

Travel Log

Introducing and using the sheet
- Ask the children what mode of transport they used to travel to their most recent holiday destination. Make a simple tally on a flip-chart.
- Ask individual children to try to remember any physical or human features passed on the way, for example rivers, seas, mountains, roads, factories or shops.
- Together look at the activity sheet and talk about each of the journeys that Gordon is to make and the features he will pass. Talk about the best way to travel to each of the destinations shown. Encourage the children to imagine that they are Gordon and then to complete the travel log.

Follow-up/extension ideas
- With the children, count the number of times that Gordon uses each form of transport. Draw a simple bar-chart using this information or the information collected from the children and displayed on the flip-chart about how they travelled to their holiday destinations.

Weather Report

- Underline the weather information in Gordon's postcards to 2B.
- In the box next to each postcard, draw a symbol to show the weather each place is having.

Souvenir

- Look at each collection of things Gordon has brought back from his holidays.
- Say where each collection is from. Use the list below.

Lake District
Paris
Spain
Austria

Travel Log

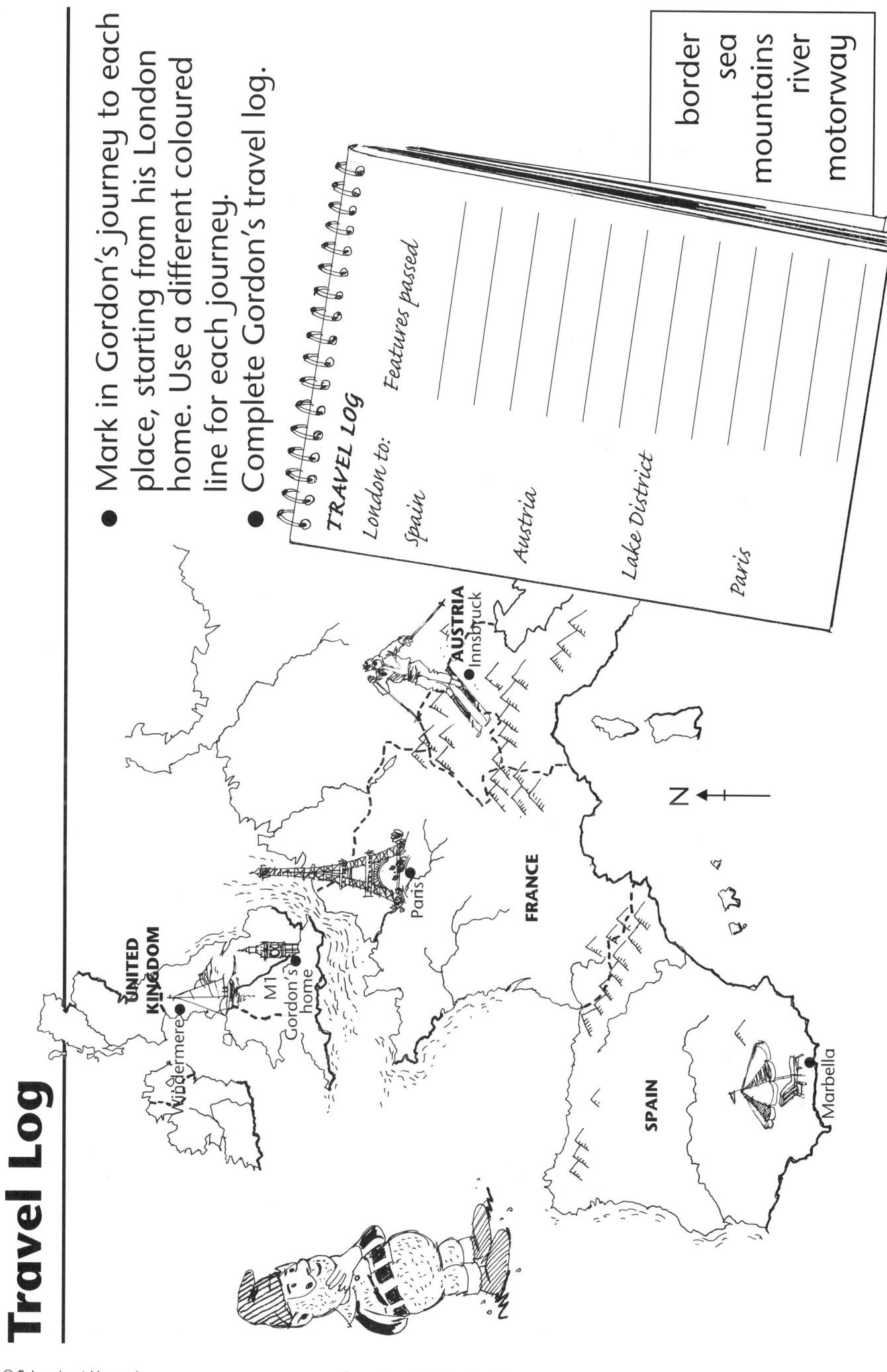

ideas page

Global Eye

Background

This unit seeks to integrate geographical method and enquiry skills with other subjects, especially Science, ICT, Design and Technology, and Personal and Social Education. It considers the sense of sight and the importance of recycling what we no longer need.

Blind Man's Buff requires the children to use plans and directions to help 'blind' people navigate their way around a house. **Visionary** shows how eyesight can be affected by the use of lenses. **See More Clearly** considers recycling old spectacles.

Learning Objectives

- To think about how useful the eye is.
- To investigate how sight can be changed using lenses.
- To consider the importance of recycling.
- To appreciate how spectacles can change people's lives.

Blind Man's Buff

Introducing and using the sheet

- Ask the children to close their eyes and notice how they can still hear, feel, smell and sense the other children. Talk about blind people and how they manage at home and in the street to find their way around safely.
- Display some words of direction: left, right, up, down, forwards, backwards, across.
- Enlarge page 41 to A3 size. Pretend to be partially sighted and ask the children to help you navigate the rooms without bumping into furniture. Begin by putting the point of your pencil on a particular spot and ask the children to direct you. Trace a line according to their directions. Then ask the children to try the activity in pairs.

Follow-up/extension ideas

- Talk about the difficulties the children had with the activity. How many times did they bump into furniture? Did they confuse left and right?
- Repeat the activity as a class: on the floor of the hall place large sheets of labelled paper to represent furniture. Again, one child is blindfolded while another gives instructions. Introduce a competitive element by adding a set course. An adult should be close to the 'blind' child to avoid accidents.

Visionary

Introducing and using the sheet

You will need a magnifying glass, a pair of binoculars and a pair of strong glasses.

- Ask an adult to talk to the children about what it is like to wear spectacles or contact lenses, and the difficulties they face when they do not have them.
- Talk about how lenses, binoculars and telescopes help us see objects more clearly. Provide a variety of lenses for the children to look through.
- Introduce the activity sheet. Cut out the 'measure' to ensure the test is fair.

Follow-up/extension ideas

- Enlarge the eye chart on page 48 and test the eyesight of volunteers. They could try and compare different lenses.
- You might link this work with a study of the eye and the in-built lens that helps us to see detail.

See More Clearly

Introducing and using the sheet

- Discuss how different aids can make us see more clearly. Many of the class may wear spectacles; some for reading, some to correct a 'lazy' eye. Do any of the children have tinted lenses to help them with reading?
- Ask the children why they think detectives are often seen with a magnifying glass. When might someone use binoculars or a telescope?
- Discuss how in economically developing countries people often cannot afford spectacles. How might our old spectacles be used to help these people?

Follow-up/extension ideas

- Spectacles and glasses do not only help us see better, they also protect our eyes. Discuss the kind of glasses we wear in bright sunlight. How else do we protect our eyes? [Wearing a hat or eye-shade; carrying a sunshade.] Discuss the kinds of protection used for different people and jobs. What might be found on a baby's pram to block out sun? Why might a fire-fighter, scientist or builder wear goggles?

Blind Man's Buff

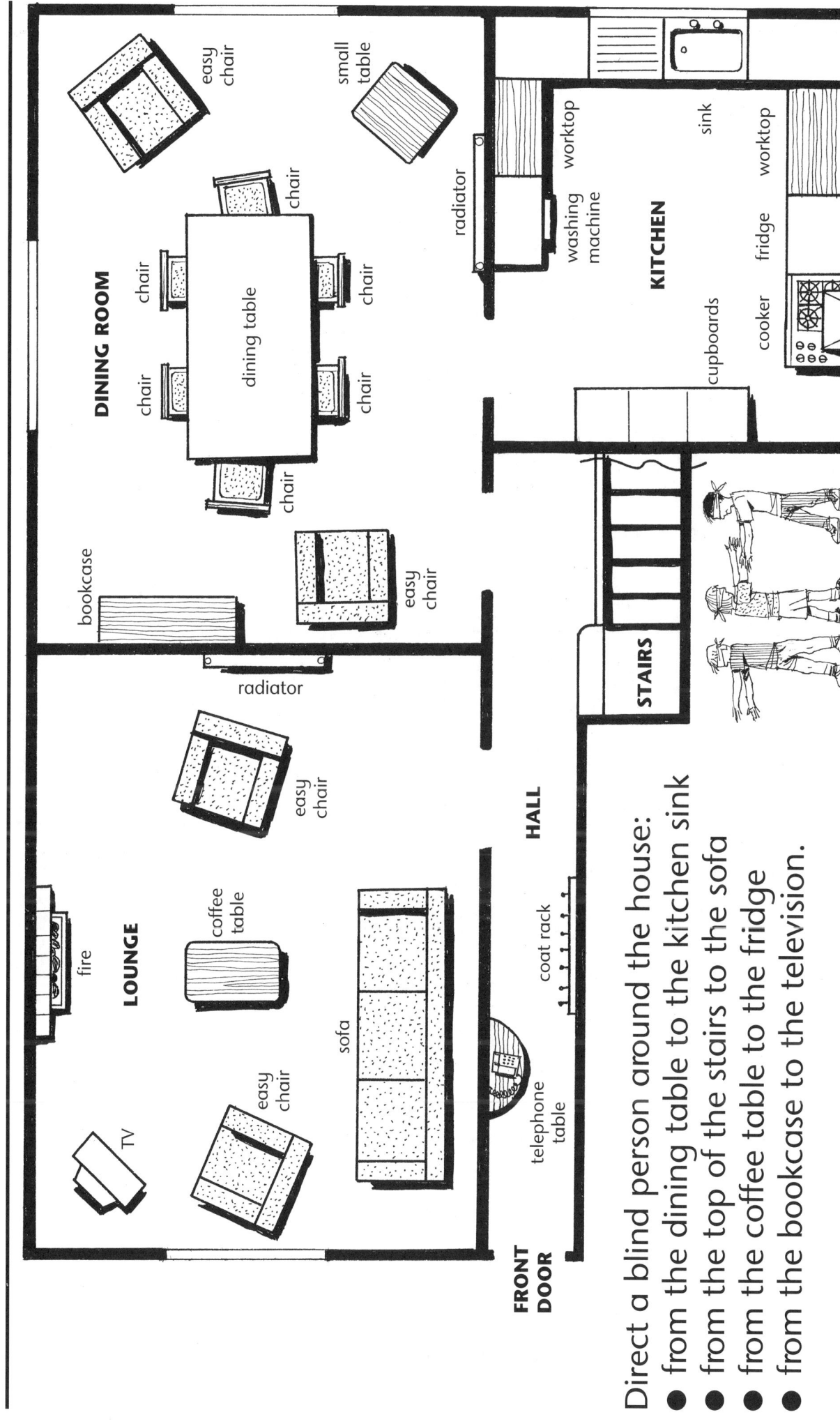

Direct a blind person around the house:
- from the dining table to the kitchen sink
- from the top of the stairs to the sofa
- from the coffee table to the fridge
- from the bookcase to the television.

© Folens (copiable page)   Geography Highlights for Infants   41

Visionary

1.

A
D E
X H Y U
N L A B U H M
D F R T O Z P G W L Q

What can you see?

2.

U
X N
P S O H
R W C L E T V
M Z X A Y R N L P F B

What can you see?

3.

H
N R
U J K F
L G N G O B A
E D S W Q X L I H C T

What can you see?

- Look at the eye-test charts through each of the lenses shown. Use the measure to make sure you are the same distance away for each test. Ask a friend to help.
- Write down what you can see each time.

EYE-TEST MEASURE 0cm — 10cm

See More Clearly

- Complete the sentences.

Spectacles help us to

A magnifying glass is used to

Binoculars are helpful for

ideas page

An Island Overseas

Background

This unit introduces a holiday locality in the Mediterranean – the island of Crete – and complements earlier work on holidays. A similar approach can be used to carry out a small-scale case study of a distant locality in a developing country. Children are encouraged to make comparisons with places they know well. The activity sheets cover travelling to Crete, the layout and nature of George's Town (Georgeoupolis), and introduce Greek customs and lifestyles through the Papadakis family.

Learning Objectives

- To locate places on a map.
- To identify physical and human features on a field sketch.
- To use secondary sources.
- To note similarities and differences between places and lifestyles.

Crete

Introducing and using the sheet
- Talk about where the island of Crete is and the best way to get there. Encourage the children to think about how difficult it would be to drive there compared with flying. Discuss how long the journey would take.
- Look at the activity sheet and talk through the route of the aeroplane flying from Manchester or London to Chania (pronounced Hania) in Crete. The children should trace the route with their fingers as you speak. Name the places that the aeroplane flies over [Manchester, Birmingham, London, Dijon, Geneva, Milan, Naples, Zakinthos, Chania]. Ask the children to label them.

Follow-up/extension ideas
- Help the children to find out more about the landscape and history of Crete, using books, software, the Internet and a good, large map of the island.
- Help pairs of children to find Chania in a good atlas and say what they think it would be like there.

George's Town

Introducing and using the sheet
- Put the children into pairs and hand out copies of the activity sheet. Encourage them to describe George's Town and the countryside around it. You may need to help them identify specific features.
- Help each pair to label some of the physical and human features in and around the town.

Follow-up/extension ideas
- Encourage the children to imagine they are walking through George's Town from the left of the sheet to the right. Ask them, in their pairs, to write down the things they see, hear and smell and to list some differences between George's Town and their home environment. Talk about their lists in a class discussion.

All Greek to Me!

Introducing and using the sheet
- The children will need a range of resources to complete the activity sheet, including books, holiday brochures on Greece, software and the Internet.
- Look at the sheet and discuss each member of the Papadakis family. Remind the children of the work covered in earlier units. What might the jobs of the family members be? How might they move about the island? What might the weather be?
- Using a flip-chart, condense what the children have been able to find out from their research into simple sentences under each topic heading. The children may then complete the sheet by copying an appropriate sentence into each box.

Follow-up/extension ideas
- Look at Greek food in reference or cookery books. Try some of the easier recipes, or copy them out to make decorated menus and display with pictures of food.
- Invite a Greek person to talk about the subjects on the sheet. Perhaps the visitor could give additional information about Crete.
- Conduct a study of another Mediterranean island such as Malta or Sicily.

Crete

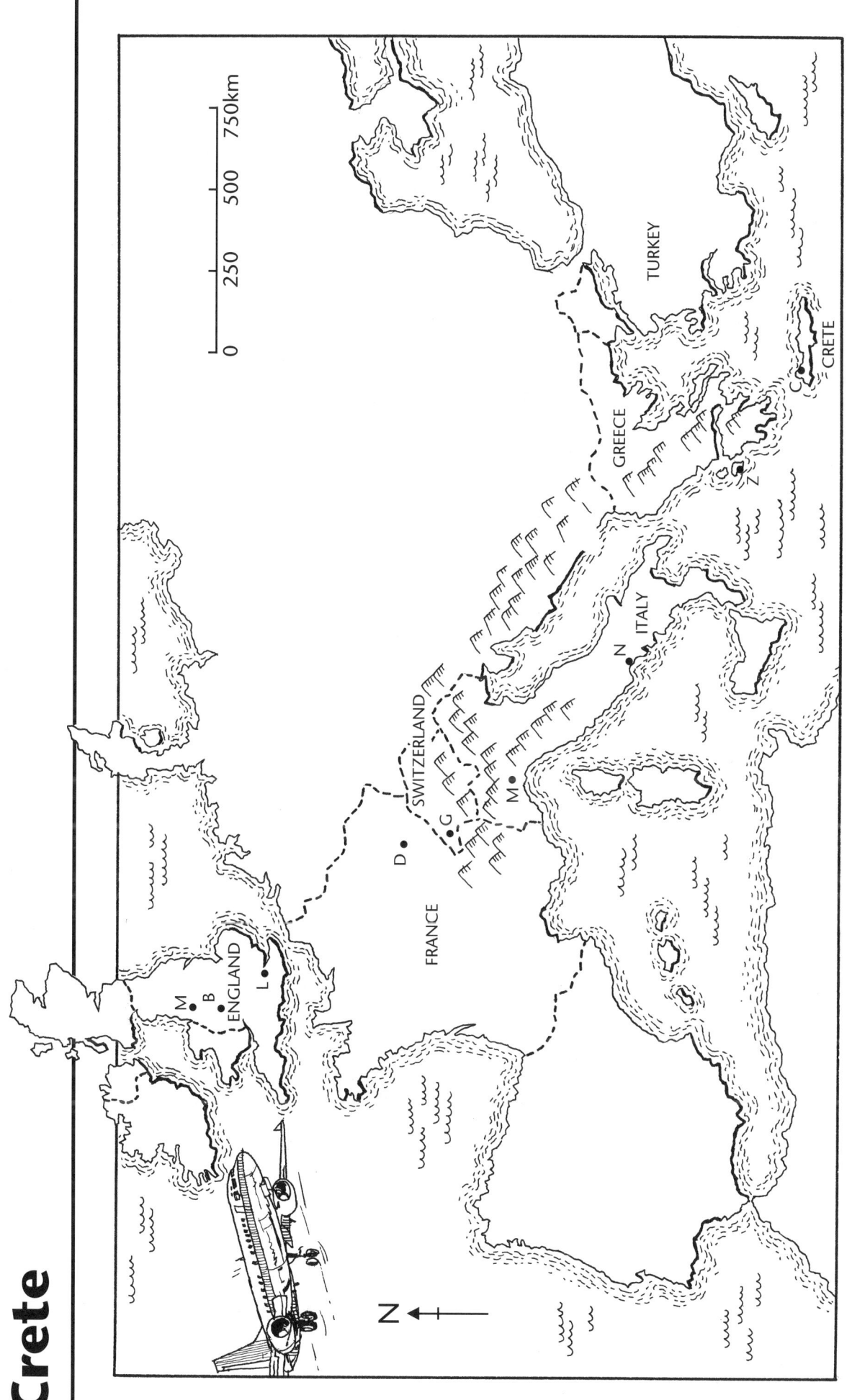

- Trace the route of the aeroplane from Manchester in England to Chania in Crete.
- Label the places marked with dots. The first letter of their names is given to help you.

George's Town

- Look carefully at George's Town and locate the features listed below. Colour each in as you find it.

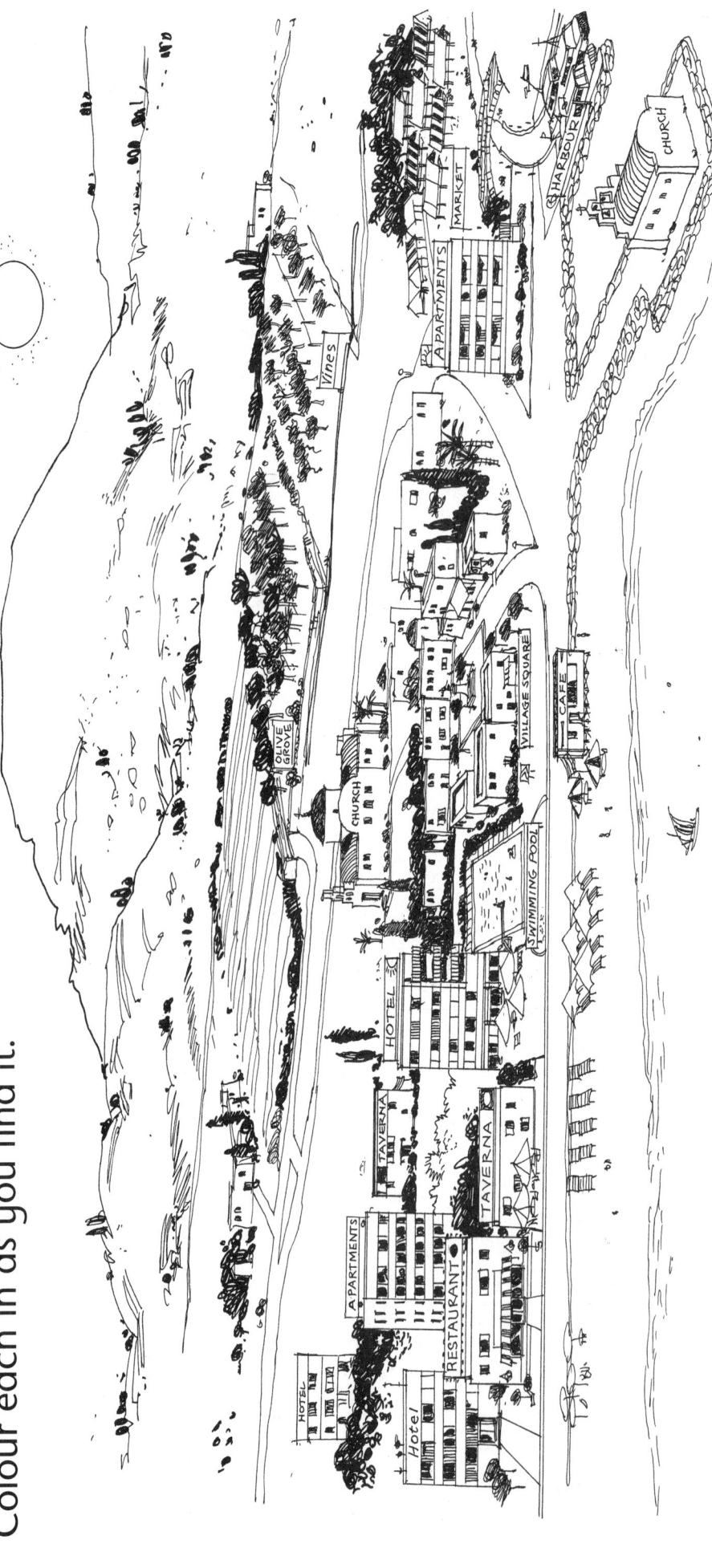

| church | mountains | harbour | road | beach | sea | village square |
| swimming pool | | olive groves | | market | | |

All Greek to Me!

| food | weather |

| Why do people go to Greece? |  |

| school | jobs |

- Find out as much information as you can about Greek life and think about what it might be like for the Papadakis family.
- Fill in each box with a sentence about the subject at the top.

Geography Highlights for Infants

Additional Information

Weather symbols

 sunshine

 snow

 hail

 heavy rain

 showers

 light cloud

 heavy cloud

 sunny intervals

 heavy cloud with sunny intervals

 lightning

 snow showers

 snow showers with sunny intervals

Eye chart

A

D X

P R V Q

T I H S N C O

Y W O F J B M L K